EPIPHANIES

NANDINI PALVE

ISBN 979-888521119-2

To Mum, Dad, Advait and Jojo, my whole heart.

To Aarya, my sister, my illustrator, without your art the book would have always been incomplete.

To you, who picked up this book, I am so grateful.

Contents

Foreword *ix*

Preface *xi*

Hurt

1. Fantods 3
2. Antagonist 5
3. Dolour 7
4. Quaintrelle 9
5. Saoirse 11
6. ☁ 13
7. Evanescent 14
8. Woe 16
9. Mishanter 19
10. Marionette 22
11. Façade 24
12. Halcyon 26
13. Melancholy 28
14. ☁ 30
15. Chagrin 31
16. Eccedentiast 33
17. Treacherous 35
18. Solace 37
19. Ostensible 39
20. Altruistic 41
21. Ramshackle 43
22. Wabi-sabi 45

Healing

Contents

23. Epiphany 49

24. Revival 51

25. Metanoia 54

26. Resilience 56

27. ☁ 58

28. Retrouvaille 59

29. ☁ 62

30. Ameliorate 63

31. ☁ 65

32. Minutiae 66

33. ☁ 68

34. Exhortation 69

35. ☁ 72

36. Formidable 73

37. Orenda 75

38. Sedulity 77

Home

39. Elysian 81

40. Archangel 84

41. Virago 86

42. Selcouth 88

43. Serendipity 90

44. Nepenthe 92

45. Rantipole 95

46. Kalopsia 97

47. Meliorism 99

Contents

48. Cordiform 101

49. Ethereal 104

❀ 107

Helplines 109

Foreword

No poet should set store by public acclamation.

Ecstatic praise will pass, an instant in the ear. The empty crowd will laugh, the fool will have his oration. But you must stay quite calm, unbending and austere.

Writing is hard, even for authors who do it all the time. They often get stuck or find a muddle on their screens and then blame themselves. What should be easy and flowing looks tangled and feeble or overblown. What's wrong with me, they all think.

But not my student, Nandini Palve. She has always been clear and sure about what she wanted. Hard work and perseverance are her passwords.

I have known Nandini since she stepped in the kindergarten of our school till she graduated to explore new avenues. She was always competitive and focused but I never knew this young naive dame will one day turn into a poetess too alongside being an engineer. Today, as I write this foreword my heart pours out the best wishes to this budding damsel.

Mrs Bharti Bijwe

Principal,

Sandipani School, Nagpur, Maharashtra, India

Preface

I didn't write these poems with the sole purpose of publishing.

These poems were written at a certain time, when I felt something twist and change inside me. It took me three years to complete this collection of poems.

This is a scary thing for me but it is kind of relieving knowing that every thought I had among these years is written down out in the open now.

It took a lot of courage; these poems were all I had. I found comfort in these words; they were my escape.

To everyone reading, I hope you find comfort in these words too.

There are a lot of things to get sad about in this world but I want you to know that you're not alone in this hurt.

Find solace in your friends and your family, confide in them.

I assure you; they want you to speak to them.

A lot happened since I wrote the first poem.

I have gotten better, life's better.

If you too feel uncomfortable right now then you're probably on the right track.

This uncomfortable journey has led me to love myself and find myself amongst everything.

This journey has led me to embrace myself.

You are all on your journeys.

I wish you peace and epiphanies.

"It is a thousand pities never to say what one feels"

-Virginia Woolf

hurt

1. Fantods

State of extreme anxiety, distress.

Fantods

I wonder if all I'll ever see is the plastic stars stuck on my roof
I wonder if someday I step outside my life
Do I get to meet the people who let me escape my past?
Or do I accept my past and move ahead
I wonder do the stars shine really that bright, that it makes us smile
Do I see the good in the people?
Will I be able to see the truth?
Do people really cross their boundaries for love?
The plastic stars are pretty in their own way,
Still, they are mere replicas
Just like the lives we choose to follow
I wonder do I get to step aside from the intricately carved path.
The stars stuck on my roof have an expiration date though
Their shine wears off, day by day, year by year
That's the thing about perfectly designed paths
They're made to reflect others
No wonder the plastic stars only shine,
When they absorb light
Unlike the stars in the sky
Who shine their own light.

2. Antagonist

An adversary

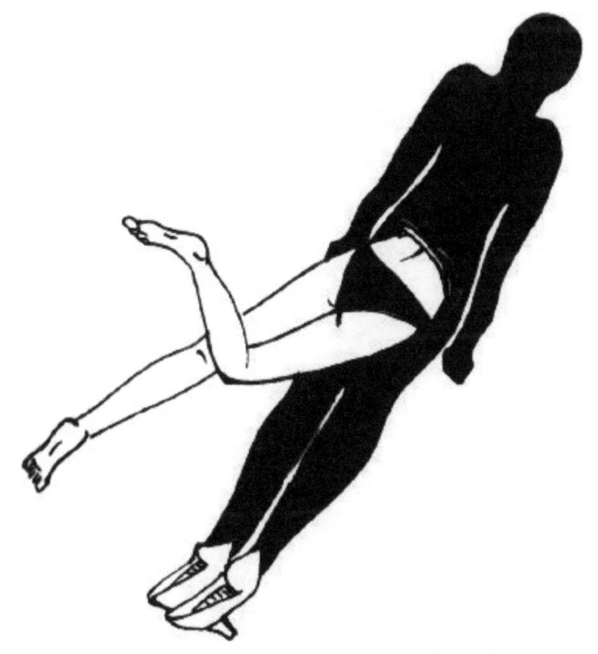

Antagonist

The day I met my villain
She didn't wear a black cloak nor did she have tiny horns neither did she carry a trident
Rather she wore a smile, a much too recognizable smile
Eyes, those eyes gazed upon me sending a chill down my spine
She did look formidable, yet comfortable
I looked at my catastrophe, she looked at her victim
I clearly know why she turned out like this
Flashbacks of her memories replay in my head
Her ailing voice echoes in my mind
There I glanced at my past mistakes and my future faults
There I was staring at my downfall
The villain of my life was no one else
But my own self

3. Dolour

A state of great sorrow or distress

Dolour

This feeling never fades
This feeling of never being enough for the people you love.
This feeling of drowning in the abyss all day all new night
How does is stop
Does it ever really stop?
Or does it stop you all along
Does it wreck your bones; tangle your head and heart?
Tell me.
When will I ever feel okay?
I‘m not asking for good
I'm just asking for okay
Don't I deserve even that much?

4. Quaintrelle

A woman who emphasizes a life of passion, expressed through personal style, leisurely pastimes, charm, and cultivation of life's pleasures.

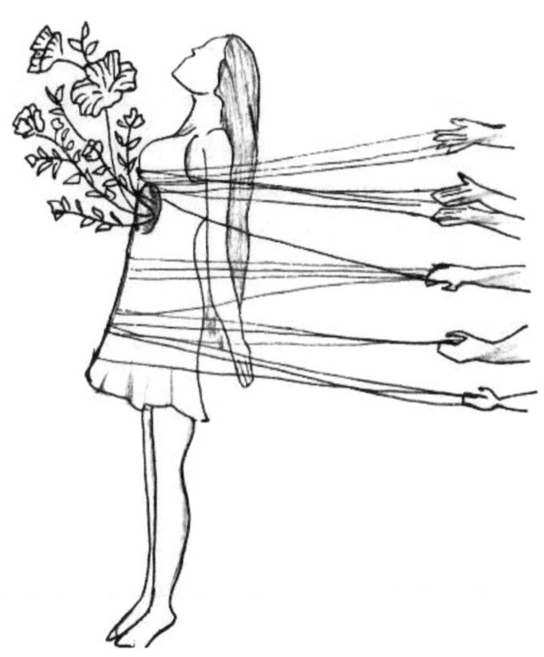

Quaintrelle

That's the point you know, you never get her
You thought she was drizzle
which you could handle
But she is a hurricane,
A tornado wrapped up in skin and caged by bones
You thought you could tame her
But her soul wasn't to be tamed
You were supposed to run wild with her
But you wanted to own her
You wanted to capture her
She loved you, she gave in to you
She thought you were worth her soul, her mind and herself
You were far more interested in her until you got her.
Then you labeled her as yours but never loved her as your own
Oh boy you tried capturing a wild child
And now you go lamenting,
Why it destroyed the both of you

5. Saoirse

liberty, freedom

❧❧❧

Saoirse

I'm wearing shiny clothes hoping to kill my dark thoughts.
But has it ever? They creep their way from my brain to my heart making their way through the luminance of the sequins on my chest.
So, I wear shiny makeup all over my body to make myself feel alive but as I glance in the mirror, I can still see the dead girl living a lie called life.
I try opening my mouth to eat, the feeling is absurd when all my life it's been shut and has only opened to put food in my stomach which rarely works because my body has decided not to accept it.
I try opening it to let my thoughts escape my mind into the air but there's silence except the sound of my screeching bones howling with contempt.
The day I'm able to step out of these castle bound heights of a place supposed to be a home I know I'd fly far away because that day you'd know a cage of comforting hands is still a cage.
That day you'd know why caged birds still sing.

6. ☁

"He was like a childhood memory; you don't quite remember did it actually happen but you can feel it deep in your bones"

7. Evanescent

Tending to vanish like vapor

Evanescent

I am standing on the ledge.

One step forward and it's the end. The voices will stop, people will stop, and life will stop. End to everything. No commas. A full stop.

One step backwards, meaning stepping again in the labyrinth of suffering. Yet I am confused. Yet I am perplexed, my dilemma haunts me.

I know jumping off will mean I ran away and I'm weak but I have been strong too long, surviving.

I am sick of all this. Just sick. I fear being alone.

Isolation, one of my greatest fears. Yet solitude is what I face the most.

Candescence of suffering never began because it never ended. It's been there all along.

How many more times do I need to drown when I only intend to swim.

How many more times do in need to fall in the deep dark abyss just to be rescued by none but myself?

Everything affects everything she said. Is this a universal thing? Or am I insane?

8. Woe

Great sorrow or distress

Woe

There is an acquaintance of mine, named Sadness.
She visits often, sometimes alone, sometimes with some friends.
We share a distant bond; I crave her presence some days, some days I am frustrated by her.
She's pretty poetry, almost known by everyone.
She is the one people write about.
She makes me question my life, my worth and my will to live.
Some days when she arrives with her friends, the five of them,
Regret, Guilt, Anxiety, Depression and her, all they talk about is the guy named Memories.
Regret has no real connection with Memories but she often wonders "What if she had a chance?"
Anxiety is a pathetic flirt with him
Guilt shares a bad past with Memories.
And as for Depression all I have ever heard her say is "I don't care".
Sadness loves blabbing about how bad Memories is and how good he was.
But I also know a girl named Joy.
Many people pretend to know her, but she in reality is known by a few
And I bless her presence to everyone who knows Sadness.
She has connections with Memories too, but my dear Sadness never talks of them.
Joy sometimes comes by herself.

Some days I need to call her unlike Sadness who comes any given moment.

They both are so different, yet so similar.

And I think I wouldn't be myself if it just wasn't for them.

9. Mishanter

Scottish

Mishap or misadventure

Mishanter

She sits in the corner. Quiet
All by herself, sitting in solitude
Smiles sometimes, thinking about the good days
Sometimes when I look at her
Her eyes are teary, but water doesn't trickle down her cheeks
She blinks away her tears
She doesn't look up she's lost in her mind
I see her zoning out
Another moment she starts writing, scribbling
I see the slits on her hands
She's not okay as she pretends to be
Her eyes are sunken, still she smiles
Her eyes say something, her smile hides it
Should I call out? should I ask her?
Two days pass her desk is empty
Her mother pulls up, she sobs as
Her husband comforts her, his shoulders slouched
The teacher informs the wounds this time were too deep
I should have asked.

10. Marionette

A puppet worked by strings.

Marionette

I have the touch opposite to Midas
Of turning golf into ash, beautiful into ruin, white to black
My skin might be soft but these scars run deeper than my veins
My fingers ache for a longing, a feeling long lost
My mind, a swirling vertex of entropy
My heart, for you, I grieve the most .
Living in mayhem, surviving was the only choice
I cherish the flowers from a distance
But that never meant I can't pluck them off their roots, to satisfy the devil's voice that echoes in my mind's darkest hallways.
The devil's words soothe me.
Remain to others no more than a disturbing voice.

11. Façade

A deceptive outward appearance.

Facade

When I was younger
I was afraid of the dark
I would run and scream as soon as the lights went off
I couldn't stand the darkness, the hollowness
I was scared of monsters
Their gruesome features and their urge to kill always terrified me
But now as I am older
How do I run away, where do I run away?
When my own mind is a dark place
Who do I call when my heart has a void?
How do I scream when the monster in my mind takes my voice away?
How do I hear my own thoughts when all I can hear is the demon whispering in the back of my mind?
How do I trust when monsters really are people?

12. Halcyon

A period of time in the past that was idyllically happy and peaceful

❧❧❧

Halcyon

It was a perfect place
Till we grew up
The heart broke,
The memories all blurred
The love all gone
And friendships are just an anecdote
The lies are pretty and everybody chants them
We live in a place where love is rationalized
Heartbreak is romanticized
Crimes are sensationalized
Rebellions are glamorized
Bad habits are glorified
And kindness is sidelined
It's getting harder to breathe each passing day
The society's stereotypes pollute the city
Worthless is no longer trash
Worthless, the people are being tagged "slut, whore, skank and prude"
Still often they wonder why the suicide rates are so high
Girls are sick but you want them to be thick
The world could've been pretty if we empathized.

13. Melancholy

A feeling of pensive sadness, typically with no obvious cause.

Melancholy

Maybe I hate myself a little too much
But maybe I'm worth it
I feel a little too numb
The smile's fake and I don't shed tears anymore
How long is it to see myself smile again?
Maybe if I look back at photographs
I could see when my smile hid the pain in my eyes
Maybe when I look at them
I'd know when I started to fade
Maybe it's the way of life
That you love someone who was never worth it
My life could be a tragic story
But maybe its poetry
As the poetess would love to believe

14. ☁

“He lived in the city where the sun won’t set and I was a traveler who loved sunsets”

15. Chagrin

Feel distressed or humiliated

Chagrin

I'm not necessarily happy right now
But I am alive
I am alive. Oh I am alive
The spirits of my scars
Still haunt me when,
I am awake or I am sleeping
The scars on my skin
Still linger in my mind
Oh how they whisper to me
Whisper their woes to my brain
My brain is not very kind
But it always hears their stories
My heart on the other hand breaks and aches
When you call me pretty
I hear just a pretty face
Can you call me a poet?
I go by artist now
My words died with the older me
Will I be able to just bring them back?

16. Eccedentiast

One who fakes a smile.

Eccedentiast

There are a million words dying to get out
But my smile plastered across my face
Shuts them out
The voice living in my head
Doesn't feel mine anymore
It screams, it howls and it laughs at me
Its words spread in my veins like poison
And I wanna sit and crumble right here
And I can't because the pain has reached beyond my bones
I can't because it's seeping through my ribcage to my heart
My heart pumps this poisoned blood all through me
It aches and it aches
I feel myself feeling this
But my mouth still curves the perfect smile I can
I know my eyes can't lie
Can you look me in the eye?

17. Treacherous

Guilty of or involving betrayal or deception.

Treacherous

I should have known
You were no exception
But I was naive
You promised me things you shouldn't have
And made me believe there was still sunshine
But too much sunshine was never good
The flowers are wilting, the earth looks barren
I'm right there where I started
I thought you held my hand
Wanting to hold it forever
But you left as soon as the dark winds whirled
You told me we'd withstand the storms together
You cursed him for leaving me broken
Now should I curse you?

18. Solace

Comfort or consolation

Solace

I have grown so fond of sadness now
That I seek comfort in it
I have felt warmth in its cold.
We're no longer only acquaintances
We have seen each other in phases
Like the earth views the moon
She's seen me be humane; I have seen her make people inhuman
She wraps her hands around me
Every day, every night, every dusk and every dawn
She's seen me grow fond of her
She's made peace with me now
We smile
We breathe
We coexist
I live, she lives within
The world maybe a mighty stranger
At least with her it is not nightmarish

19. Ostensible

Stated or appearing to be true but not necessarily so

Ostensible

Her love for you was always the same
You were the moon, changing
loving her in phases.
But the moon is too cliché
to have any flaws
So, you blamed it on her
Called her a paradoxical idea
You told your night time lovers,
She was a beauty one moment
At the another a hurricane,
Destroying hearts that came in her way
Sure, was she a hurricane for your drizzle like love which quenched the thirst of your
night time fillers
But her happiness lied in your star drunk eyes, your constellation of thoughts.
Maybe she is to blame
Maybe the joke's on her
But you, you grew flowers in heart,
And watched her suffocate under them.

20. Altruistic

Showing a disinterested and selfless concern for the well-being of others; unselfish

Altruistic

Look how I drown
Look how I drown in my own thoughts
Look how I jump into deep waters even though I can't swim
Look how I drown in the river of tears
Look how I breathe even though the water is up to my mouth.
Look how I drown saving others
Look how I hustle
Look how the water makes me clean

21. Ramshackle

Appearing ready to collapse

Ramshackle

At that exact moment
It fell crashing down
The world swirled
My hands shuddered
My voice quavered
It was no longer a high-pitched bubbly voice
I spoke words, softly placing them one by one
My feelings were a kaleidoscope of emptiness, guilt and regret
I knew I didn't do good living
I felt like a burden on those with me and around me
I wanted to have a good cry, let it off my chest
But I felt numb
I felt like a poem without a soul
I wanted it to stop
Me, my life and my world
My castle fell way too many times
I am sick
I am sick of rebuilding it again and yet again
The sun would still shine
The moon will still rise
I don't know if I'm still alive

22. Wabi-sabi

A concept, an aesthetic and a world view that focuses on finding beauty within the imperfections of life and accepting peacefully the cycle of growth and decay.

Wabi-sabi

We all are broken
Broken in our hearts
Broken in our minds
And broken in our thoughts
Searching for someone with the
same broken piece like ours
To heal the wound and bury the mark
But the world is too broken
for the exchange of sympathy and empathy
And the people are too shy
to show their scars
Now tell me how do we expect
to lift each other's soul when we don't even know
If the other is happy, crying or dying inside
When we all are lost inside the world we carry in our hearts
How are we supposed to see the magnificent world outside
when we are blinded by our own trauma?

healing

23. Epiphany

A moment of sudden and great revelation or realization

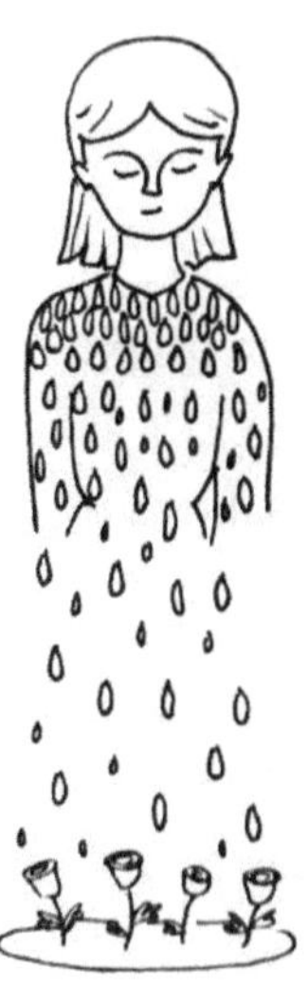

Epiphany

As a little girl I overwatered the plants
I didn't know when to stop giving,
A little older I poured my heart out for half truths,
I didn't know when to stop giving
I held onto the rope a little tighter so that the
other would not fall, regardless of the
bruises I came along.
I never knew when to stop giving
As I grew older, I sought refuge in people,
They sought me as a resting place.
A place to visit during restless nights and
monotonous days
My empathy and their apathy
My naive heart and their leery mind was a lethal combination.
It took me 17 years to realize that
people aren't medicine.
We ourselves are.
The disease and the cure
It's all in us

24. Revival

An improvement in the condition, strength, or fortunes of someone or something

Revival

I look in the mirror,
I see two selves of mine distort
I see the Princess, whining
I see her breaking, crying
I see knives stabbed in her back
She wails, she fails
She smiles, she cries.
Then I see the other move,
The Queen walks in poise
Her head held high
With her boundaries set and her weird flex
She is Coffee, she is Contour
She is Confident
She lends out a hand to the little girl
Makes her stand up on her feet
Bandages her wounds
Helps her straighten the crown
I see them
Standing tall, with fire in their eyes
I see them
I feel the rage in their voice
I see them
With change in their choice
I look at the little girl
I see me
I look at the Queen
I feel me

I look at the Queen in the becoming
I feel her
She's better than before
I'm her.

25. Metanoia

Change in one's way of life resulting from penitence or spiritual conversion.

❧❧❧

Metanoia

She has changed you can see it in her eyes. She has changed she doesn't believe it though; always goes around doubting herself, but she can clearly feel it in her soul. You can see it when she smiles so beautifully from her heart. A real smile not like the smile she used to fake before. That smile was like a weapon she used to hide all her pain. She doesn't feel empty anymore, she feels a million capacities spring up inside her. Her thoughts before were a chaos, haunting her, making her rush into unjust and stupid acts which sure made her happy but were superficial and at last proved detrimental. But not anymore, she can now hear her own voice, guiding her, comforting her and assuring her. She sometimes thinks this person is just a mere stranger. But she knows that she had always longed to be this person. This person who is not just pretty but beautiful, this person who speaks her heart without hesitating, this person who is not arrogant. This girl who is truly happy, this girl who lives in the now. And this daughter who loves her parents more than anything else. This is who she wanted to be and I think she slowly is. This is her Metanoia.

26. Resilience

The capacity to recover quickly from difficulties; toughness.

Resilience

I'm drawing these flowers on my skin
Flowers, waves, leaves, birds
I'm drawing and drawing
I'm doing this so I don't slit
tonight
I'm trying to calm my breath
My hands, my legs all scribbled
Calm down I whisper to myself
Calm down
The voice inside my brain says
Do it. Do it. Do it
I'm fighting against it
Fight, fight, fight
I'm a warrior
I'm a warrior
I'm a warrior
My body's a mess now
At least my brain is shushed
I'm okay tonight
I fought this
I did it tonight

27.

"Tragedies happen and do come the betrayals. When they arrive our minds and hearts are shattered. We believe in things in which we had no faith before and lose hope in beautiful things of our own. When these nasty things come free to us in our lives, we consider all of it was our fault and blind ourselves from seeing the truth. We believe that each atom of our existence is worthless. But oh, my darling this is wrong, somethings do happen on which you have no control upon. Somethings just reach their deadline. But for somethings in your life, you yourselves can choose the deadline. Don't stop living because others won't let you. If they say you can't, just prove 'em wrong. You have been assigned this mountain to show the world that it can be moved."

28. Retrouvaille

The joy of meeting or finding someone again after a long separation; rediscovery

Retrouvaille

Who am I
It's that uneasy question which
makes me feel uncanny
Who am I
I like to see the good in people,
But l would like to know the truth after all
Nobody likes half-truths
that's what they told me at least
I like to believe I'm carbon and bad
timing
Who am I
I would say I'm a poem with no soul
The problem is that I sometimes feel a little too much
And mostly I don't even know what I
feel
Is it heartache or betrayal
Who am I
Do I miss somebody? I don't know.
I shouldn't miss people who broke
my heart, that's what I need to keep
in mind, my friends told me.
Who am I
l am all the women I read
Sylvia, Emily, Virginia,
Anne, Harriet, Harper

Who am I
I am all the girls
Who cried their heart out
I'm all the people who believe love's
the cure to this one heck of a world.
Who am I
A daughter, a friend,
A sinner, an angel,
A lover, a cheater
Betrayer, betrayed
The good, the bad
A poem, a formula
The history, the past
The present, the future
Who am I
I'm yet to find
All I know is that
I'm everything except
I'm not nothing
I want you to believe that too.

29.

"There are so many theories out there of love, of friendship, of heartbreak and of betrayal. You study each one of them, hear different versions of the same story but you never come across the truth, you just pick up one to whom you feel a lot comfortable with, then someday you experience these things all by yourself, then you have your own theory"

30. Ameliorate

Make something unsatisfactory better

Ameliorate

I have had ups and I have had my downs
I have been the light; I have stolen away darkness
And I have been the darkness and I have stolen light
I have been the victim and I have played the victim
I have been a prisoner to my heart
I have stayed in its clutches way beyond my sentence
I have weaved words, sung poems for it
I have carried the chains of it into my present
But I won't
I won't anymore, I don't want to anymore
I have made mistakes and there's no going back now
But I have found the key to these chains
I forgive myself; I forgive the ones who wronged me
I liberate myself from this vicious cycle of self-hate, regret and pity
I might be free but I'm still grounded
I walk on the path carved by these lessons
Learnt the hard way.
For today and everyday
I breath, I exist, I am.

31. ☁

"Memories are often black and white, there are no grey ones because they aren't worth remembering"

32. Minutiae

The small, precise, or trivial details of something.

Minutiae

It always doesn't have to be a rainy Sunday afternoon, it could be a windy Wednesday morning, a thundering Tuesday night or a mild Monday afternoon but for me it was a showering Saturday evening when I felt beyond my past, beyond my mistakes, beyond the drama
I no longer felt like a broken dream I felt like a mosaic stitched together by faith and hope
Some pieces were lost, some stolen
But I knew I'd complete my masterpiece by better ones.
I stitched my cracks by golden threads. Someone I know said to me I didn't feel like myself lately
But believe me honey I have never felt more of me

33.

"Now you know, I understand that heart breaks, people leave, promises break, beautiful starts have ugly endings. But all I know is that rough times pass, it sure does take a hell lot of time but they pass, and once the storm passes you won't really remember how you managed to make it to through, you won't know that the storm has really passed or not but I know one thing for sure, that you won't be the person as the one who walked in the storm"

34. Exhortation

An address or communication emphatically urging someone to do something.

Exhortation

If I meet my 13 year old self
I'll tell her little girl,
Cherish the moment when your mother looks at you proudly
Till the time you are 17, time changes
I'll tell her, when her best friend tells her she loves you
Believe her innocence
I'll tell her to choose herself instead of the guy with the sly smile
I'll tell her to not be afraid to smile because it's the prettiest and the realest thing she could ever have
I'll warn her that she'll fake the smiles later
I'll watch her be the life of the party, only later to avoid them
I'll convince her to believe that she is enough and their words don't matter
I'll hold her hand, be her shoulder, and tell her she has to be cold
I'll warn her, she'll bruise herself saving people
I want to tell her people can't be made into homes
I want to tell her to save some pieces of herself before they are all lost
Because right now I don't have a clue who I am
I want her to know I tried to be happy
I want her to know I tried killing my sadness
I want her to know people leave without an explanation leaving you here gasping for air,
I want her to know, if I could, I would tell myself at 13 that she'll get lied to.
But most of all,

I want her to know
You survive all this
You are a warrior
I'm so proud of you
Nobody else might be, but I am and always will be.

35. ☁

"Pieces of poetry fit your soul tell them you're not a damsel in distress to be saved by those"

36. Formidable

Inspiring fear or respect through being impressively large, powerful, intense, or capable.

Formidable

They told you to start a war, to be a strong warrior queen
But I don't think you need to start a war
Every woman is fighting a bloody war with her body; there is no need to start another
You can start a revolution, be a revolutionary queen and be the kind of queen they envy.
The queen who is impossible to defeat.
Become that.
Be that girl

37. Orenda

A supernatural, divine force within every human being. Always omnipresent. It empowers people to change the world in a positive, loving way.

"At the end, everybody needs someone who goes out of their way to save them, but it is okay to save ourselves"

"I know you want to save somebody, but you know the world is too messed up and complicated and everybody is not as simple as they seem to be and there is a reason why everybody turns out a certain way and how so many people prefer wearing masks, but let me tell you one thing that by understanding the simple complexity of the world you saved yourself"

38. Sedulity

The quality of being constantly diligent and attentive

Sedulity

I was born a December girl
So you'd think I'd know when the last chapter was near
But winter creeps in slowly and I almost never see it coming
One days it's fall and I'm drinking pumpkin spice latte and lighting lamps for the festive season
Next morning, I feel the breeze, hitting me like a cold shoulder
Fall's long gone
And you've stopped falling for me
Winter's here and I no longer have you to keep me warm
It's 9 December today
I know you won't come back to warm me up
So I burn the flowers you sent me to ignite a fire.
December's ending so I know spring is close.
Next spring, I'll grow flowers in my own garden

home

39. Elysian

Beautiful or creative; divinely inspired; peaceful and perfect.

Elysian

You don't know her, do you?
You think she is pretty poetry, But she's a sad one.
She's a warrior, she fights the demons inside her, yet she tries to save everyone.
She's a wreck, but she is a mosaic.
She stitches her pieces together to create the beautiful masterpiece she is.
She lives in phases.
She is the moon.
I am the moon.
I am her.

40. Archangel

An angel of greater than ordinary rank.

Archangel

Was losing friends, then I got you
You cried when I was half asleep and slept when I was wide awake
Woke up me up with your tongue licking my face
And how could I or anyone else not give in to that little angel face of yours
The way you come running, tap tap tapping your little fuzzy paws
That gleam in your eyes when people call you a
good girl.
You really are the best girl
Every day I wake up and see you wagging your tail
You're my greatest teacher
I'm the one with all the words
People still never understood me
But you do
I might fail to understand your woofs.
But you, you look me in the eye and you know when to lie down on my lap.
My angel, I'll always be grateful for you

41. Virago

A female warrior.

Virago

To the girls born with stubborn hearts,
I know exactly how it felt when your right went wrong
I have the clue how hard it is to trust because,
Apparently, your conscience lied to you
I know you tried to scrap off your skin, your thoughts
Your past, I know it still sends a shiver down your spine
I know people stopped talking shit about you
But your mighty brain still whispers those words to your messy heart
I know the world's a dark place and you're scared to let go off your guard
But you, you are a warrior, you be the light in these dark places
Be the bright place, we are destined to be the light.
No, I won't ask you to put others first
I won't ask you to break yourself for others, No I won't
This time I want you to put yourself first
Your heart is a masterpiece wrapped up in chaos
This time my warrior queen, you have to save yourself
I know I know you have the habit of putting people you love above you
But I would like to ask you a question,
How long will it take for you to stumble across your name when you list the names of the people you love?
I want you to put yours first
I know you want to save someone
This time let that be you
- We are not damsels in distress
We are goddesses

42. Selcouth

Unfamiliar, rare, strange and yet marvelous

Selcouth

She's a wreck
She's art
She's what you don't see
You don't understand, she's more than what you think
She's heartbreak
She's the song you don't know the quotes you haven't read, the words you don't speak
You have no idea what lies inside her
The more she speaks, the more you fall in love
Listen to her carefully you'll know her story
Look at her carefully; you'll know what she feels
When she's down, her eyes won't shine
It will be difficult to get a word out of her
When she's happy she'll make you happy
She'll giggle, she'll smile
She's a mess, a language you haven't learnt
I'm a mess, I'm heartache
My heart isn't mine, still it lets me live
I'm a novel, a haiku, a song, a poem
A collapsed miracle, a distressed soul
A dying star, the moon, the sun, the stars, a nebula
I'm her

43. Serendipity

Finding something good without looking for it

Serendipity

They wanted me to write about love
So, I wrote about heartache
Write about growth they insisted
I scribbled about decay.
There's something poetic about heartache and decay that binds people together.
Love and growth come eventually
Decay and heartache arrive at your doorstep as a stranger
It takes time to get acquainted with strangers
That's what shatters people
As decay reveals people, heartache breaks them
Both of them at once lead to destruction
Then you find yourself wrapped in your lover's hands, begging them to make it stop
This is how I knew I loved you
Amidst the chaos
There was you.

44. Nepenthe

A drug mentioned in the Odyssey as a remedy for grief.

Nepenthe

When you're young,
We think of love with irrational expectations,
Love at first time, is what you think you want.
Red roses and candle lights
As the years pass and the night changes
Sometimes you find love online.
A stranger.
A stranger who flips your world upside down
A love that starts with friendship and memes.
A different kind of love.
When people ask you, how did you two meet?
You don't get to tell them, our eyes crossed in a cafe
Rather you tell them
He texted me to set me up with his friend.
I know you're an old soul
But sometimes, this modern love, sweeps you off your feet.
I know you wanted to find love in your first ever relationship
Things perish easily these days.
I know you called yourself a sad prose
This love makes you feel like singing your heart out to the cliché choruses
This love is sunflowers and roasting each other
I know you thought you'd fall in love with someone completely different.
But this love makes your write happy verses
This love helps you grow.
This love makes you love yourself.

I know this is new for you.
Sometimes love greets you as a best friend.

45. Rantipole

Wild, reckless young person

Rantipole

You go baby girl,
We are granddaughters of the witches they couldn't burn.
We run this world
You have stardust in your veins
Millions of stars collided to have you in this world at this particular time.
Don't let their sacrifice to go in vain.
You are a miracle, a beautiful one.
A work of art and a piece of poetry written at 2 A.M ,when the whole world is asleep but a creative mind is buzzing, soaring high up in the sky.
You can't be fitted in some cheesy words; you deserve a whole series written in your name.
Don't let this shitty world stop you.
Remember only the dead fish go with the flow.

46. Kalopsia

The delusion of things being more beautiful than they really are

Kalopsia

Now I know how she is
She is like sweet coffee
She is strong, but her sweetness overshadows her darkness
Yes, she is exactly like coffee
Her presence always lifts my soul, my body and my mind altogether.

47. Meliorism

The belief that the world gets better; the belief that humans can improve the world.

Meliorism

I have a thing for people who are undeniably themselves, who are recklessly honest, who follow their hearts
I am in love with these people
Who are determined to change the world and save it.
I fall for those people who love hard, who love unconditionally, and who love selflessly
My heart aches for them, who've got a fighting spirit and who are hustlers
I am completely in love with these people
because a bit of each of them resides in me, though vague but still in an infinite feeling

48. Cordiform

Heart shaped

❧❧❧

Cordiform

We're in the car,
I look out of the window, the wind flowing
through my hair,
I see the trees move, thinking about how many moments passed
bringing us to this now.
I see him
One hand on the steering wheel
One on my hand.
We are in the car,
I see her gazing out of the window,
The sunshine makes you notice her golden strands.
The moment feels like it's scented with summertime
Life has been so much better since her,
it's happy, it is fun
I hold her hand and I realize one thing
"It's not where I go; it's who I go with"
I blast our favourite song, I look at him.
His eyes are on the road.
Mine on him
I watch him steal glances of me
We smile with our eyes
I feel the daylight in my veins
This love feels golden
I look at her smiling like an idiot looking at me
Singing our favourite songs, I hold her hand tightly
Her aura is made of poetry, daisies and the galaxy
We were together and everything else was forgotten

I can see it, this is it
This is what I want forever.

49. Ethereal

Extremely delicate and light in a way that seems not to be of this world

Ethereal

We didn't find love one day.
It wasn't some Sunday morning
Nor was it some thundering Thursday
You slowly, helped me put down the
bricks in my fortress
It wasn't a sentence. It wasn't an action
It wasn't a Hollywood movie
This was it
You slowly carved your way in my heart.
You hugged my heart and told my head to calm itself.
They both agreed, I couldn't do that
myself all these years.
I might be a hurricane
You are an earthquake
Shaking my grounds
The belief system I had about love
You tossed it out.
I might be winter; you are my summer.
You brought spring in my life
Maybe someday I will too.

"All the hurt in my heart is art now"

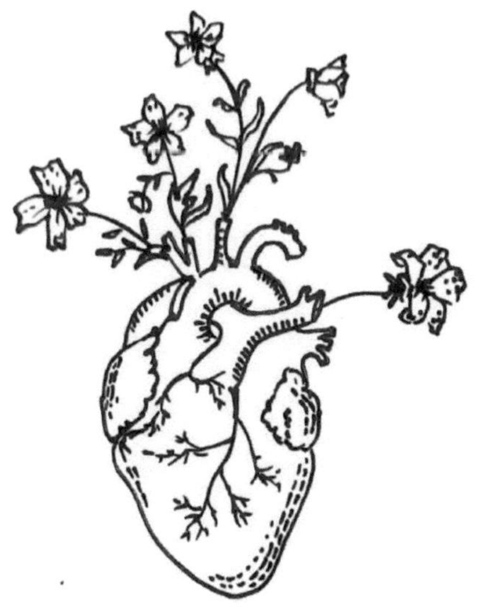

Helplines

These Suicide Helplines Can Be Of Assistance In Times Of Need

1. Roshni

1. **Where**: Plot Number 326, Laxmi Nilayam, 2nd Lane, Landmark: Near Grand Kakatiya Hotel, Hyderabad
2. **When**: Monday to Saturday, 10 AM to 7 PM
3. **Contact**: +914066202000
4. **Email**: roshnihelp@gmail.com

2. Sneha India Foundation

1. **Where**: 11, Park View Road, Krishnapuri, Raja Annamalai Puram, Chennai, Tamil Nadu
2. **When**: 24x7
3. **Contact**: 044 2464 0050
4. **Email**: help@snehaindia.org

3. Aasra

1. **Where**: 104, Sunrise Arcade, Plot No. 100, Sector 16, Koparkhairane,

Navi Mumbai

2. **When**: 24x7
3. **Contact**: 022 2754 6669
4. **Email**: aasrahelpline@yahoo.com

4. Arpita Foundation

1. **Where**: HBR 2nd stage extension, 3rd main road, Arabic college post, Bangalore
2. **When**: Monday to Sunday, 2:00 PM to 5:00 PM
3. **Contact**: 011- 23655557
4. **Email**: arpita.helpline@gmail.com

5. Sanjivini Society for Mental Health

1. **Where**: H Block North, Under Defence Colony Flyover, Jangpura Side, New Delhi
2. **When**: Monday to Friday, 10:00 AM to 5:30 PM
3. **Contact**: +911124311918
4. **Email**: sanjivini1971@gmail.com

6. iCALL

1. **Where**: V.N. Purav Marg, Eden Gardens, Deonar, Mumbai
2. **When**: Monday to Saturday, 8:00 AM to 10:00 PM
3. **Contact**: 022-25521111
4. **Email**: icall@tiss.ed

7. *Snehi*

1. **Where**: B-140, 1st Floor, Vasant Kunj Enclave, Delhi
2. **When**: Open on all days, 2:00 PM to 6:00 PM
3. **Contact**: 011-26521415
4. **Email:** info@snehi.org, snehi.india@gmail.com

8. *Samaritans Mumbai*

1. **Where**: 402, Jasmine, Opposite Kala Kendra, Dadasaheb Phalke Road, Dadar (E) Mumbai
2. **When**: Open on all days, 3:00 PM to 9:00 PM
3. **Contact**:+91 84229 84528, +91 84229 84529, +91 84229 84530
4. **Email**: amaritans.helpline@gmail.com

9. *Vandrevala Foundation*

1. **Where:** Present virtually. Admin Office - 5th Floor, Supreme Business

Park, Powai, Mumbai

2. **24x7 National & International Helpline Number:** +919999666555
3. **24x7 Email Id:** help@vandrevalafoundation.com

Printed by Libri Plureos GmbH in Hamburg,
Germany